Contents

Introduction 5
Blackline Masters
draw 1, 2
Review 3, 4, 5, 6
under 7
Review 8, 9, 10
by 11
Review 12, 13, 14, 15, 16, 17, 18, 19
house 20
Review 21, 22, 23
mouse 24
Review 25, 26, 27, 28, 29
orange, oranges 30
Review 31, 32
is 33
Review 34, 35, 36, 37
not 38
Review 39, 40
can 41
Review 42, 43
cannot 44
Review 45, 46
yes, no 47
Review 48, 49
girl 50, 51
boy 52
Review 53, 54, 55, 56
play 57, 58
jump 59, 60
run 61
Review 62, 63, 64, 65
duck 66
Review 67, 68

truck 69
Review 70, 71
in 72
Review 73, 74, 75, 76, 77, 78
go 79
fast 80
Review 81, 82
up 83, 84
down 85
Review 86, 87, 88
hill 89
Review 90, 91
dog 92
Review 93, 94
treehouse 95
playhouse 96
doghouse 97
Review 98
will 99
Review 100, 101
this 102, 103
pond 104, 105
sand 106
grass 107
Review 108, 109, 110, 111, 112
get 113
wet 114, 115
to 116, 117
into 118, 119
mother 120
father 121
Review 122–128

The Cove Phonics Program

Introduction

Mastery of the alphabetic principle of reading—that is, recognizing the correspondence of symbol to sound—is essential for a student's progress toward reading independence. Direct instruction in this skill is especially important for students with weak phonological skills who have not yet developed the ability to perceive separate sounds in words or to segment words into natural spoken syllables. Such students might have dyslexia and/or other learning disabilities, they might be children from impoverished language environments, or they might be those considered at risk for formal instruction. Students learning English as a second language can also benefit. Many of these students might be discouraged and eventually overwhelmed by a too-rapid progression to new material or by sketchy and insufficient instruction.

The Cove Phonics Program was designed to provide the teacher with an organized, sequential phonics-based reading program. It consists of a phonics inventory to help the teacher determine the appropriate placement of the student in the program, eight workbooks for learning symbol-sound correspondence, mastery lists for developing automatic word recognition, and fiction and nonfiction reading selections for applying reading skills as they are mastered.

For young students whose visual-perceptual and visual-memory skills are relatively well developed, but whose phonological readiness for direct phonics instruction is weak, there is a set of materials for learning by sight. These materials, *Getting Ready for Phonics,* are suitable for use while phonological awareness is being taught, before beginning work in the *Consonants Workbook,* or in conjunction with that workbook. Other students may begin directly with one of the workbooks, depending upon the results of the phonics inventory.

The Cove Phonics Program is the culmination of extensive classroom experience, chiefly with dyslexic and other learning disabled students. The program is written by Joyce Dadouche and Janis Wennberg, both former Cove School teachers and currently private tutors, and Laura Rogan, co-founder and former Clinical Director of Cove School. The authors are presently with the Cove Foundation, a not-for-profit organization engaged in the development of educational materials and research for children and adults with learning disabilities or at risk for academic failure. The Foundation is an outgrowth of the Cove School, which was founded in 1947. It was the first school to meet the needs of students with dyslexia and other learning disabilities.

The materials can be used by students working independently in a classroom situation or as a group. The organization of the lessons and the vocabulary help develop the students' confidence and independent study habits by allowing the students to work with minimal teacher assistance. With some modifications, most of the materials can be used with students at any age or grade level.

Components of The Cove Phonics Program

Program Guide

The Cove Phonics Program Guide contains suggestions for using the program, a Phonics Inventory, and Performance Records.

The purpose of the Phonics Inventory is to establish each student's approximate level of functional phonics knowledge for appropriate instruction. It consists of a Primary Inventory of single letters and digraphs and seven other inventories of phonically regular words. There are two forms of each inventory, except the Primary Inventory, to correspond with each workbook.

You should administer a Form A inventory, or several Form A inventories, before selecting a workbook for a student. You can record the results on the Performance Record. The inventories can also be used to monitor progress after an appropriate interval of instruction. For post-instruction testing, use Form B to measure progress.

Getting Ready for Phonics

These two sets of worksheets are appropriately used with young or immature children who are not yet ready for direct phonics instruction. Common words are taught as whole words through a variety of exercises, such as matching, coloring, and cutting and pasting. An effort has been made to select words with clearly perceived consonant and vowel sounds that will help to lay the foundation for later phonics work. Some children will benefit most by beginning with these worksheets before using the *Consonants Workbook*. Others may use the worksheets and the *Consonants Workbook*, or even the *Short Vowels Workbook*, at the same time. Still others, like many children with dyslexia, will be more successful by beginning with the *Consonants Workbook* and skipping the *Getting Ready for Phonics* worksheets.

The format is simple, minimizing the need for teacher explanation and allowing for independent work and self instruction. Pictures are clear and easy to identify. There is ample spacing between words in a sentence and lines of text. Practice in manual coordination, small muscle use, and organization is provided by the cutting and pasting exercises. The child with well-developed writing skills may write the word in the spaces.

Cove Phonics Teacher's Guides

In addition to directions for using the workbook pages, the Teacher's Guides contain an answer key to the exercises in the student workbooks; Word Lists that you can use in games, in individual or group exercises, or on flash cards; Mastery Lists with instructions; and Practice Readers on blackline masters that cover the phonetic elements the students have practiced in their workbooks. The Mastery Lists and Practice Readers are on blackline masters.

Practice in developing automaticity of response in word recognition should accompany work in each of the workbooks. Studies have shown that reading fluency contributes significantly to reading comprehension; lack of automaticity, even though the reader can "sound out" the words, leads to a slower reading rate that can adversely affect understanding. Mastery Lists, coordinated with the workbook pages, assist in developing automaticity.

Throughout the process of learning to read, the student needs opportunities to apply developing skills. The most effective reading material will be consistent with the student's level of decoding ability. Practice reading material is included in *The Cove Phonics Program* with every workbook except the *Consonants Workbook*. This reading material permits reading practice directly correlated to the phonics instruction in the workbook. The stories and articles, therefore, can be read with relative ease by students who have mastered the current and preceding workbook lessons. Because the student is not interrupted or frustrated by words he or she cannot read, the student experiences the direct benefit and pleasure of reading interesting material virtually without assistance.

The Cove Phonics Workbooks

The workbooks in *The Cove Phonics Program* are the primary tool for developing recognition of symbol-sound correspondence for single letters, letter clusters, and letter patterns and for practice in combining the separate sounds into meaningful words and sentences. The sentences are composed almost entirely of the target words and words containing previously taught phonic patterns. The very few words with irregular spellings are taught as sight words. This vocabulary control ensures that the student will not be prevented from working independently because of words he or she cannot read. The knowledge of phonic principles and vocabulary is cumulative because of the abundant natural review provided by the carefully selected vocabulary.

New material is presented gradually with frequent reviews. Material is well spaced on a page, and the illustrations are simple and easy to identify. Because writing is important in helping strengthen memory for symbol-sound associations and words, most of the lessons require some writing.

The first five workbooks do not include instructions for the student to read because of inherent problems with the vocabulary required. Beginning with the *Long Vowels Workbook* short, simple directions are given for the learner, using many of the phonic patterns already mastered by the student. Because the lesson formats are simple, the learners will quickly recognize the task with very little guidance from the teacher.

Consonants Workbook

The *Consonants Workbook* establishs symbol-sound relationships of consonants.

The order in which the first few consonants (*m, t, p, k, j, f*) are presented corresponds to the ease with which they can be discriminated auditorily. In most instances, the lip, tongue, and mouth positions needed to form these consonants are clearly visible and easily perceived both tactually and kinesthetically.

Additional linkage between symbol and sound is formed by having the student write the letter or trace it while saying the sound. Such multisensory feedback at this early level helps form strong associations between the letters and their corresponding sounds.

Words illustrating a consonant sound have been carefully chosen so the sound is clearly perceived as a single consonant sound followed or preceded by a vowel.

Short Vowels Workbook

Because mastery of the short vowels is critical for growth in word-analysis skills, the *Short Vowels Workbook* is devoted entirely to the development of this skill.

The order in which the vowels are presented corresponds to the ease with which they can usually be differentiated auditorily from one another. This also tends to correspond to the ease with which they can be produced by the teacher and student. Thus, *a* (*apple, cat*) is first, followed by *o* (*octopus, cot*). The remaining vowels—*i* (*igloo, sit*), *u* (*up, nut*), and *e* (*egg, bed*)—are more difficult to discriminate from *a* and *o* and from each other and require subtle modifications of the oral structures in order to be produced accurately.

Each vowel is introduced separately with key pictures. The target vowel is used in three-letter words (*c-v-c*), which are contrasted with words containing previously learned vowels.

Simple contextual reading is provided in sentences using only *c-v-c* words together with very few sight words.

Consonant Blends & Digraphs, Part 1 Workbook

The *Consonant Blends & Digraphs, Part 1 Workbook* emphasizes initial consonant blends in short vowel words. Words with two final consonant blends (*st, sk*), double final consonants (*hill*), and two different final consonants sounded as one (*back*) are presented. Consonant digraphs (*sh, th, wh, ch*) and the cluster *qu*, which do require new associative learning, are also included.

Because only the five short vowels are used, the *Consonant Blends & Digraphs, Part 1 Workbook* provides reinforcement and review of the short vowels. This is particularly beneficial to the student whose response to the short vowel grapheme is still not fully automatic because it enables him or her to move on to slightly more complex material without becoming confused or overloaded.

Consonant Blends & Digraphs, Part 2 Workbook

The *Consonant Blends & Digraphs, Part 2 Workbook* advances phonics skills to final consonant blends and digraphs. Many students who have been taught initial consonants and short vowels tend to neglect the final consonant blends in their reading. Therefore, the major emphasis in this workbook is on final consonant blends and the clusters *tch*, *vowel-ng*, and *vowel-nk*. Three-letter initial consonant blends are included as are the verb ending *-ing*, compound words, and selected sight words. Initial consonant blends and short vowels are used in the lessons, providing ongoing review of these skills while developing accurate and fluent response to final consonants.

Vowel Digraphs*, Part 1 Workbook

The *Vowel Digraphs, Part 1 Workbook* has two major emphases: introducing eleven vowel digraphs, diphthongs, and vowel-consonant combinations (*ee, ea, oo, ai, ay, or, oa, ar, ou, ow, er*) and developing visual strategies for sounding out (decoding) two-syllable words.

The vocabulary in the carefully controlled sentences is cumulative; only words with short vowels, consonant blends and digraphs, and the sight words taught in the preceding workbooks are included with the new material.

*The terms *vowel digraph* and *vowel-consonant combination* are used to simplify the frequently confusing terminology used by different authorities. The terms are used to indicate a commonly occurring written letter pair to which one responds with a given sound or set of sounds.

Long Vowels Workbook

In the *Long Vowels Workbook* the approach to decoding words is more analytical because the student is required to choose which vowel sound to use. This may be based on context (*wind, find*), spelling (final *e* as the marker for the long vowel sound), and visual memory of word patterns (*boot, book, riding, toe*).

In addition to final silent *e* words, two new vowel digraphs (*oo* as in *book* and *ow* as in *snow*) and long vowel pattern words (*pie, toe, blue, most, bolt, roll, cold, find, wild*) are presented. Contractions, exceptions to the final *e* rule, and selected sight words are also given. Practice is provided in applying strategies for reading final *e* words when suffixes beginning with a vowel are added, as well as techniques for reducing two-syllable words to more manageable units.

For the first time, instructions to the student written in controlled vocabulary and simplified language are given on each page. The words used in the directions are presented as sight words and are given in a small glossary for student reference.

Vowel Digraphs, Part 2 Workbook

The seventh phonics workbook is the *Vowel Digraphs, Part 2 Workbook*. It presents more letter patterns and word analysis including two new vowel digraphs (*oi, oy*); two vowel-consonant combinations (*ur, ir*); and soft *c*, soft *g*, and silent *k* and *w*. Exercises are presented for adding *-y* and *-est* to words ending in *e* (*stone—stony, safe—safest*) and some contractions, selected sight words, and rules for possessives and plurals.

Instructions to the student, given at the top of each page, are short and simply stated.

Lessons that require the student to read words in context include sentence completion, yes/no questions, and definitions. Classification lessons and crossword puzzles provide variety.

Vowel Digraphs, Part 3 Workbook

The eighth phonics workbook is the *Vowel Digraphs, Part 3 Workbook*. It presents five new vowel digraphs (*aw, au, ey, ew, ea*); four vowel-consonant combinations (*igh, ight, aught, ought*); variant sounds for *ar*, *or*, and *er*; silent *gh*; and a number of sight words. Lessons are provided on contractions, open and closed syllables, and selected suffixes and prefixes.

Name _____

Draw   draw

| dawn | brow | draw | raw | draw |
| pawn | draw | drew | wrap | draw |

| draw | draw | draw |
| draw | draw | draw |

Name _____

Draw a box.	Draw 2 cats.
Draw a wagon.	Draw 3 bats.
Draw a big tree.	Draw a little tree.

Name _____

color	draw

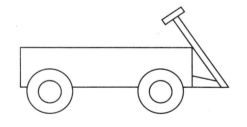  

Color the fox black.

Draw a bat on the wagon.

Draw a yellow X on the apple.

| draw | color | draw | color | draw | color |

Name _____
_____

Draw a box.
Color the box purple.
_____

Draw 3 trees.
Color 2 trees green.
_____

Draw 2 cats.
Color the cats orange.
_____

Draw 4 apples.
Color the apples red.
_____

Name _____

Draw a red X on the apple.
Draw a brown X on the tree.
Color the fox purple.
Draw a blue X on the bee.
Draw a yellow X on the fox.
Color the wagon green and black.

Name _____

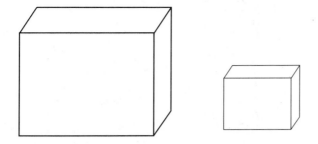

_____

Draw a cat on the big box.
Draw 2 apples on the big tree.
Draw a bee on the little box.
Draw 1 apple on the little tree.
Color the apples red.

Name _____

Under   under

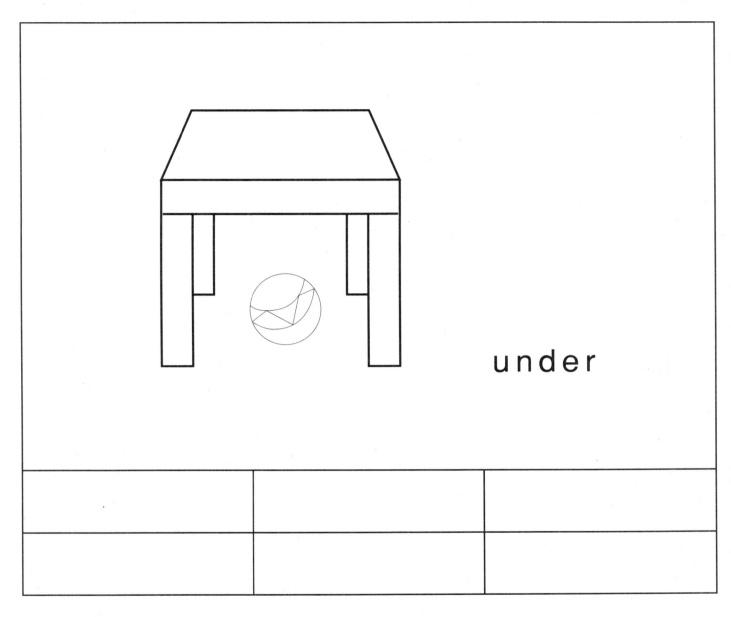

under   upper   number   under   runner
other   under   under   hunger   rung

| under | under | under |
| under | under | under |

Name_____

a box under a tree
a tree on a box

a cat on a box
a box and a cat

a fox under a tree
a fox on a tree

a bee under a wagon
a wagon under a bee

apples on a tree
apples under a tree

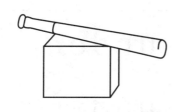

big box on a bat
big bat on a little box

Name_____

 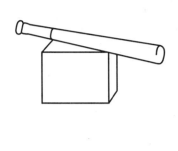 

a fox under   a tree
apples under   a box
a bat on   a bee

a tree under   a box
apples on   a tree
a big orange under   the bee

Name_____

Draw a box under the big bee.

Color the big bee yellow and black.

Color the orange under the wagon orange.

Draw a big box and a little wagon.

Name _____

By   by

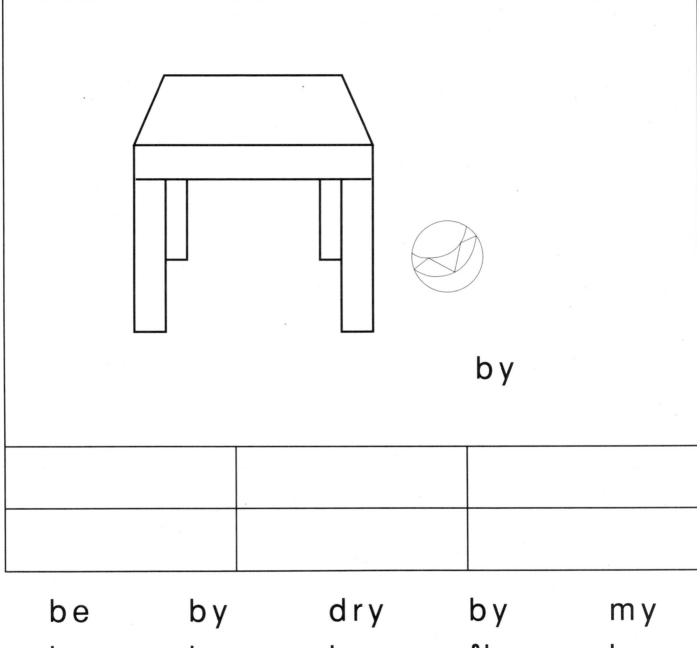

| be | by | dry | by | my |
| by | boy | bug | fly | by |

by	by	by
by	by	by

Name_____

 apple and orange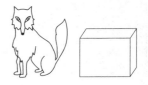

fox by a box

fox on a box

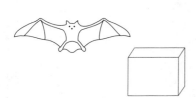 box by a bat

 apples on a tree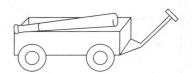

bat on a wagon

wagon and a cat

 bee by a box

Name_____

	a cat by the box a cat on the box
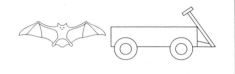	a bat on a wagon a bat by a wagon
	a tree by a box a tree on a box
	a box on a bee a bee on a box
	a bat by a cat a bat on a cat
	a fox by a cat a fox on a cat

Name _____

Color the cat by the box yellow.

Color the fox by the box brown.

Draw a big apple by the orange.

Color the little bee by the tree orange.

Color the cat by the wagon black and brown.

Draw a little wagon by the tree.

Name _____

under	by

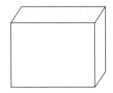 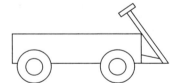 

Draw a purple X by the wagon.
Draw a blue X under the box.
Draw a yellow X on the fox.

| by | under | under | by | by | under |

Name _____

under   by

under   by

under   by

under   by

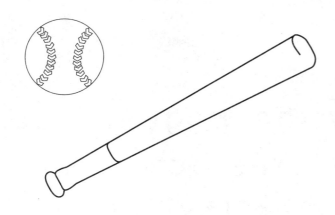

under   by

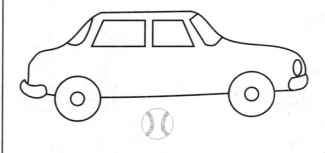

under   by

Getting Ready for Phonics Part 2. Permission is granted to reproduce for classroom use.

Name_____

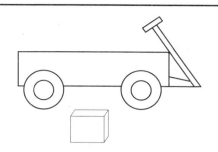 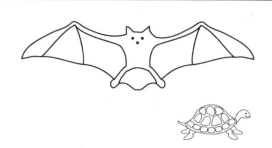

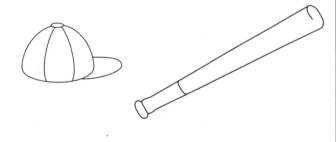 

under the box	under the wagon
under the bat	by the box
by the wagon	by the bat

Name_____

a cat ☐ the fox	a bat ☐ a box
a fox ☐ a box	a bee ☐ the apple
a box ☐ a cat	a fox ☐ a bee

| under | on | on | by | under | by |

18/128   *Getting Ready for Phonics Part 2.* Permission is granted to reproduce for classroom use.   Copyright © 1995 SRA/McGraw-Hill.

Name_____

I see a ☐ on the tree.

I see a ☐ under the bat.

I see a ☐ by the tree.

I see the ☐ on a wagon.

I see a ☐ under the tree.

I see a ☐ by the box.

| wagon | cat | box | fox | bee | apple |

Name_____

House   house

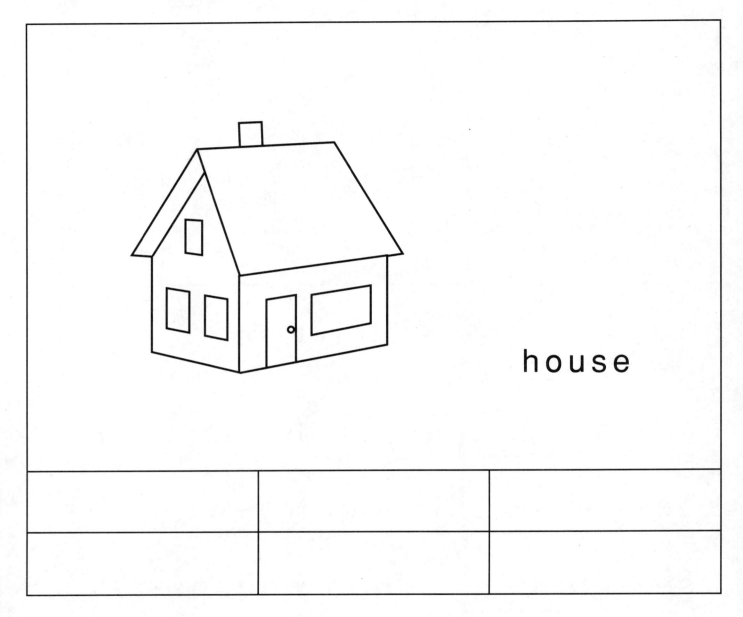

hour   house   mouse   south   house
hose   house   house   ounce   nose

house	house	house
house	house	house

20/128   Getting Ready for Phonics Part 2. Permission is granted to reproduce for classroom use.   Copyright © 1995 SRA/McGraw-Hill.

Name_____

a tree by
a bee on
oranges under

the house
a tree
a cat

big apples
a little fox
a little wagon

by a house
on a tree
under a box

21/128 Getting Ready for Phonics Part 2. Permission is granted to reproduce for classroom use. Copyright © 1995 SRA/McGraw-Hill.

Name_____

I see a ☐ by the house.

I see apples on ☐ box.

The little cat sees a ☐.

The brown ☐ sees a house.

The big ☐ is by a green tree.

I see a big cat by a ☐ cat.

| bat | the | little | tree | fox | house |

Getting Ready for Phonics Part 2. Permission is granted to reproduce for classroom use. Copyright © 1995 SRA/McGraw-Hill.

Name_____

Draw a tree by the house.
Color the house orange.
Draw a cat under the tree.
Draw a bee on the house.
Color the fox black and brown.
Draw a box by the fox.

Name_____

Mouse   mouse

nose   mouse   must   mouse   noise
mouse   more   mound   nouns   mouse

| mouse | mouse | mouse |
| mouse | mouse | mouse |

Name_____

a mouse on a wagon	a house under a tree
a mouse under a wagon	a mouse on a house
a house by a wagon	a mouse by a house

Getting Ready for Phonics Part 2. Permission is granted to reproduce for classroom use.

Name_____

I see ☐ houses.

I see ☐ mouse.

I see ☐ bees.

I see ☐ apples.

I see ☐ wagons.

I see ☐ trees.

| 1 | 2 | 3 | 4 | 5 | 6 |

Name_____

Color.

I see a red house.

I see a black cat by the house.

I see 2 brown bats.

I see a green apple under the tree.

I see 3 yellow bees on the tree.

Name_____
_____

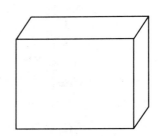

Draw a mouse on the box.
Draw a tree by the house.
Draw a cat under the big wagon.
Draw a bat by the big wagon.
Color the house purple and green.
Color the mouse black and brown.

Name_____

_____

The cat sees a _____ by the box.
       red   mouse

_____

The little brown mouse sees the big _____ .
                       color   cat

_____

I see a big _____ under the wagon.
       bee   blue

_____

I color the apples on the tree _____ .
                        the   red

_____

The black and yellow bees see a _____ .
                        tree   the

_____

I see a big red house and a _____ tree.
                     under   green

_____

The mouse _____ on the big wagon.
       sees   is

_____

The big green tree _____ by the house.
            sees   is

_____

Getting Ready for Phonics Part 2. Permission is granted to reproduce for classroom use.   Copyright © 1995 SRA/McGraw-Hill.

Name_____

(1 circle)	(2 circles)
1 orange	2 oranges

oranges   greens   sang   ranges   oranges
orders   stranger   oranges   oranges   romps

orange	oranges	orange
oranges	orange	oranges

Name_____

Color the house purple.

Color the houses blue.

Color the orange yellow.

Color the mouse brown.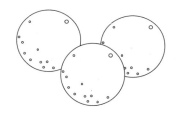

Color the apple green.

Color the oranges orange.

Color the apples red.

Name_____

Draw 3 oranges on the orange tree.

Draw 2 oranges under the tree.

Color the oranges.

Draw 4 apples on the apple tree.

Color the apples.

Draw 2 cats by the apple tree.

Color 1 cat black and 1 cat yellow.

Color the trees.

Name_____

Is   is

The cat is big.

us   as   is   sit   is   in
sip   is   it   is   his   sis

is	is	is
is	is	is

Name_____

The [ ] is by the tree.

The cat is by the [ ].

The bat is [ ] the fox.

The [ ] is on the wagon.

The box is by the [ ].

The bee [ ] big.

| fox | by | box | wagon | tree | is |

Name_____

A bee [   ] by a fox.

A mouse [   ] on a house.

The orange is [   ] a tree.

A bat is [   ] a box.

A tree [   ] by a house.

A bee is [   ] a mouse.

| is | is | is | on | by | under |

35/128 *Getting Ready for Phonics Part 2.* Permission is granted to reproduce for classroom use. Copyright © 1995 SRA/McGraw-Hill.

Name_____

The little mouse _____ on the brown box.
　　　　　　　　　is　　sees

The black cat _____ under the wagon.
　　　　　　　is　　sees

The red wagon _____ by the house.
　　　　　　　is　　sees

The fox _____ a little mouse.
　　　　is　　sees

The big box _____ orange.
　　　　　　is　　sees

The apple on the wagon _____ red.
　　　　　　　　　　　is　　sees

I _____ a purple and yellow box.
　see　　is

The black cat _____ the little mouse.
　　　　　　　sees　　is

Name_____

I see a bee on a tree.

A bee [ ] on the tree.

I see a fox by the house.

[ ] fox is [ ] the house.

I see a mouse on the box.

[ ] mouse is [ ] the box.

I see the apple by the cat.

The apple [ ] by the cat.

| by | A | is | A | is | on |

Name_____

Not   not

The mouse is not big.

on   not   ton   not   net
not   on   out   no   not

not	not	not
not	not	not

Name_____

A bee ☐ on the apple.

A cat ☐ under the box.

A tree ☐ by the house.

The orange ☐ on the box.

A fox ☐ by the house.

A bat ☐ under the wagon.

| is | is | is | is not | is not | is not |

Name _____

A mouse _____ red.
          is   is not

A _____ is not little.
  color   cat

A cat is not _____ .
           black   blue

A mouse is not _____ .
             green   brown

A _____ is not big.
  mouse   tree

A _____ is not red.
  mouse   house

A bee _____ yellow and orange.
      is   is not

A mouse _____ purple and yellow.
         is   is not

Getting Ready for Phonics Part 2. Permission is granted to reproduce for classroom use.   Copyright © 1995 SRA/McGraw-Hill.

Name_____

Can   can

can

I |can| color.

cat   can   can   car   cab
can   and   an   can   cab   man

can	can	can
can	can	can

Name_____

 I can color.

I can see the house.

The cat can see the mouse.

The cat is black.

The can is big.

The cat is by the can.

Name_____

Color the big can purple.
Draw a little can by the mouse.
Draw a black X on the little can.
Draw a cat on the big can.
Color the cat on the can yellow.
Draw a mouse by the big can.

Name_____

can   cannot

can	cannot

I _____ color.
    can   cannot

A cat _____ color.
      can   cannot

A mouse _____ see.
         can   cannot

A house _____ see.
         can   cannot

| can | cannot | can | cannot | can | cannot |

Name _____

_____

I _____ see blue oranges.
can   cannot

I _____ draw and color a tree.
can   cannot

A mouse _____ draw a tree.
can   cannot

A cat _____ see a house.
can   cannot

I _____ color a wagon red.
can   cannot

A house _____ draw a mouse.
can   cannot

A big box _____ see a little box.
can   cannot

A mouse _____ color the apple blue.
can   cannot

Name_____

A fox is
| by the box |

A little mouse is
| |

The fox cannot
| |

A bee is on
| |

The cat is not by
| |

The cat cannot
| |

the orange tree.	see the mouse.
by the box.	under the box.
the oranges.	see the bee.

Name_____

Yes   yes   No   no

yes	no
yes	no

[yes]			[no]		
say	you	yes	no	on	not
vet	yes	yam	in	no	of
yes	yet	yes	no	an	no

yes	no	no	yes	no	yes

47/128   Getting Ready for Phonics Part 2. Permission is granted to reproduce for classroom use.   Copyright © 1995 SRA/McGraw-Hill.

Name_____

Is a mouse orange?	yes no
Can a mouse draw?	yes no
Can a fox see?	yes no
Can a house see?	yes no
Is a mouse little?	yes no
Is a house big?	yes no
Is a bee purple?	yes no
Can a cat color?	yes no
Is a bee little?	yes no
Is a cat blue?	yes no

Name_____

Is the apple under the wagon?	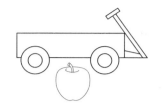	yes no
Is the mouse by the oranges?		yes no
Is the boy on the house?		yes no
Is the girl on the box?		yes no
Is the apple under the bats?	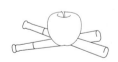	yes no
Is the fox by the tree?		yes no

Name_____

Girl   girl

| girl | grill | grin | girl | rig |
| pill | girl | girl | pull | drill |

girl	girl	girl
girl	girl	girl

Name_____

Can a girl color a wagon?	yes no
Can a girl see a mouse?	yes no
Can a mouse draw a house?	yes no
Can a girl bat?	yes no
Can I see a purple girl?	yes no
Is a little girl big?	yes no
Can a girl see a bee?	yes no
Can a girl see under a wagon?	yes no
Can a girl see a purple mouse?	yes no
Can a cat see a girl?	yes no

Getting Ready for Phonics Part 2. Permission is granted to reproduce for classroom use.

Name_____

Boy   boy

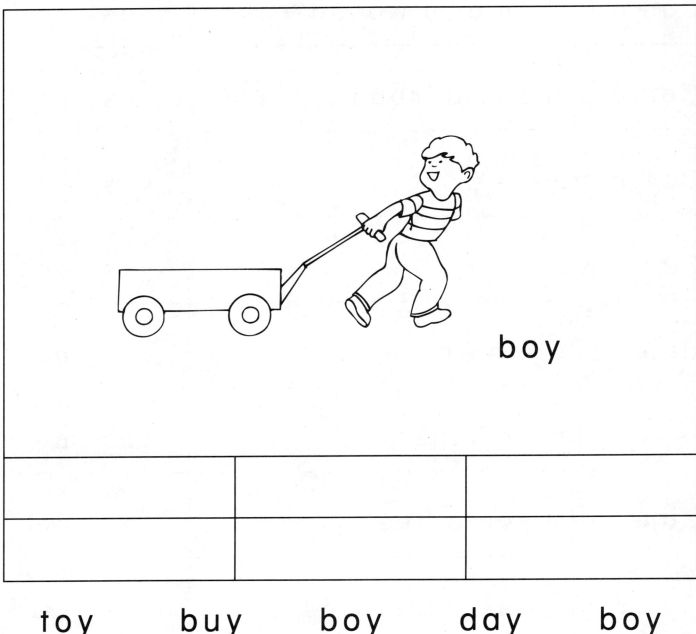

boy

toy   buy   boy   day   boy
boy   dog   yap   pay   boy

boy	boy	boy
boy	boy	boy

Name_____

The [ ] is big.

The boy can [ ].

The boy is on a [ ].

The little [ ] sees a cat.

The boy draws a [ ].

The [ ] is not by the tree.

| bat | wagon | boy | boy | boy | house |

Name_____

girl	boy

Draw a bat on the wagon.

Color the ▯ on the boy blue.

Draw a cat by the girl.

Color the 🛼 brown.

| girl | boy | boy | girl | boy | girl |

Name_____

| house | boys | mouse | houses | apples | wagon |
| girls | bees | orange | oranges | boy | girl |

Name_____

Is the boy on the house?		yes no
Is the bee by the little girl?		yes no
Is the boy on a box?		yes no
Is the mouse by the girl?		yes no
Is a girl under the big tree?		yes no
Is the boy under the orange tree?		yes no

Name_____

Play   play

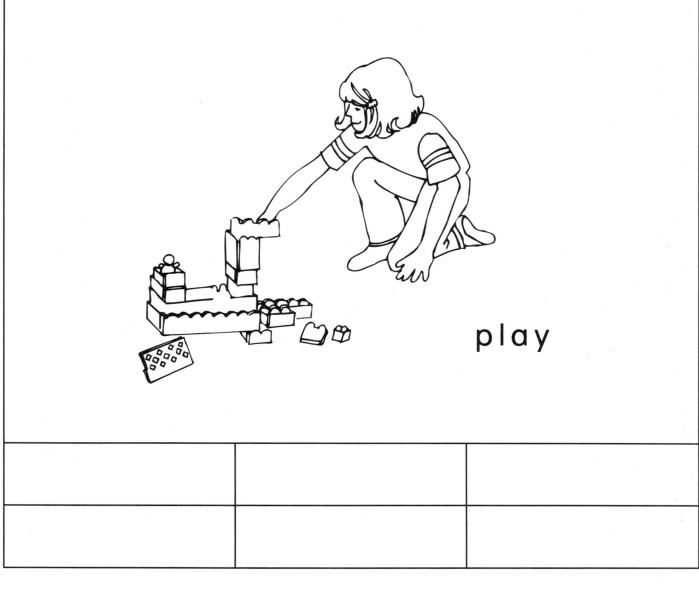

play

plan   play   lay   pay   play
yap   ploy   day   play   bay

play	play	play
play	play	play

Name_____

Can a house play?	yes no
Can a girl play?	yes no
Can a box play?	yes no
Can a fox play?	yes no
Can the mouse play house?	yes no
Can oranges play on a tree?	yes no
Can a boy and a girl play?	yes no
Can a cat play by a girl?	yes no
Can a boy play under a tree?	yes no
Can a wagon play?	yes no

Name_____

Jump   jump

jump

jump   just   chimp   pump   jump
jam   gum   jump   jump   mumps

jump	jump	jump
jump	jump	jump

Name_____

_____

A mouse _____ jump.
          can   cannot

A house cannot _____ .
                    yes   jump

A girl can _____ .
             jump   boy

A _____ can jump.
   can   cat

A fox can _____ .
             jump   draw

A _____ can draw.
   jump   girl

Apples _____ jump.
          cannot   can

A little boy can _____ a house.
                        jump   draw

Name_____

Run run

rub   nun   run   rug   run
run   nor   urn   ran   run

run	run	run
run	run	run

Name_____

 run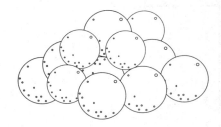

jump

 can

oranges

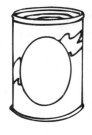 run

play

 under

run

Name_____

play	jump	run
play	jeep	run
pink	jump	red
play	just	run
purple	jump	rain
play	jump	ran
blue	jack	run

Can a girl jump? yes no
Can a boy run? yes no
Can a mouse play house? yes no
Can a cat run and jump? yes no

Name_____

Can oranges and apples play?	yes	no
Can a mouse run?	yes	no
Can a big cat jump?	yes	no
Can a girl and a boy run?	yes	no
Can a wagon jump?	yes	no
Can houses play?	yes	no
Can a bee run?	yes	no
Can a boy and a cat play?	yes	no
Can a girl run under a tree?	yes	no
Can a box jump?	yes	no

Getting Ready for Phonics Part 2. Permission is granted to reproduce for classroom use. Copyright © 1995 SRA/McGraw-Hill.

Name_____

I see a boy, a girl, and a cat.

The girl cannot play.

The boy can run and play.

The cat can jump on the 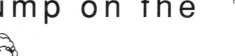 .

The girl is 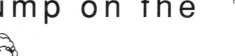 .

Can the girl play?	yes no
Can the cat jump?	yes no
Can the boy play?	yes no
Can the girl run?	yes no
Can the boy run?	yes no

Name_____

Duck   duck

dock   dunk   duck   buck   duck
duck   puck   duck   luck   lock

duck	duck	duck
duck	duck	duck

Name _____

The big duck is _____.
yes   yellow

The _____ cannot jump.
duck   boy

A duck _____ red.
is   is not

I can see a _____.
under   duck

The big duck can see a _____.
draw   fox

A mouse _____ a duck.
is   is not

A duck can _____ a little.
color   run

A _____ cannot draw a house.
girl   duck

Name_____

a cat and a duck | a duck by a tree
a duck on a box | a box on a duck
a duck and a boy | a duck on a tree

Name_____

Truck   truck

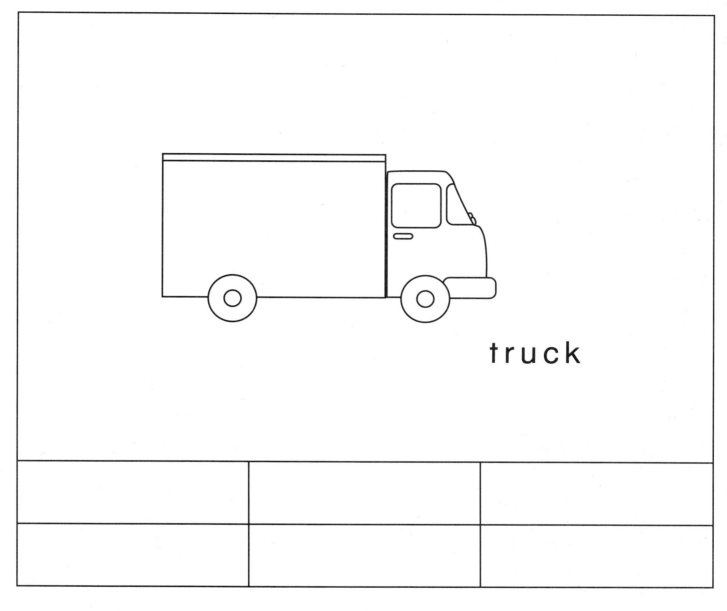

truck

truck   trick   trunk   track   truck
duck   truck   thick   truck   trust

truck	truck	truck
truck	truck	truck

Name_____

duck	truck
dock	track
duck	tree
draw	truck
black	black
duck	truck
back	brick

Is a duck blue?	yes	no
Is a truck big?	yes	no
Can a duck see?	yes	no
Can a truck draw?	yes	no

Name_____

71/128 *Getting Ready for Phonics Part 2.* Permission is granted to reproduce for classroom use.   Copyright © 1995 SRA/McGraw-Hill.

Name_____

In in

on　　in　　it　　is　　an
if　　an　　no　　in　　in

in　　　　in　　　　in
in　　　　in　　　　in

Name_____

Name_____

A truck is ☐ the box.

The mouse is ☐ the box.

A house is ☐ the box.

A girl is ☐ the wagon.

A boy is ☐ the wagon.

A duck is ☐ the wagon.

| in | in | on | by | by | under |

Name_____

A boy is in the truck.
A boy is by the truck.

A cat is under the wagon.
A cat is in the wagon.
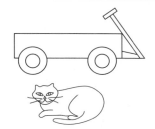

A duck is on the box.
A duck is in the box.

The truck is by the house.
The truck is in the house.

The box is on the wagon.
The box is on the truck.

A girl is by the house.
A girl is in the house.

Name_____

I see a ☐ on a house.

I see a boy in the ☐.

I see ☐ in a tree.

A big cat is under a ☐.

I see 2 little ☐ under the tree.

I see little cats in a ☐.

| wagon | tree | cats | apples | mouse | house |

Name_____

Color the duck in the wagon yellow.
Color the duck on the wagon brown.
Color the box in the truck black.
Color the box by the truck blue.
Draw a girl by the truck.
Draw a boy by the wagon.

Name_____

The little girl is under the _____.
                                                        truck   tree

The big girl can _____.
                            jump   run

The boy _____ in a truck.
                 is   is not

The truck _____ play.
                 can   cannot

The truck is _____ the tree.
                 up   under

The _____ cannot run.
             girl   truck

Name_____

Go   go

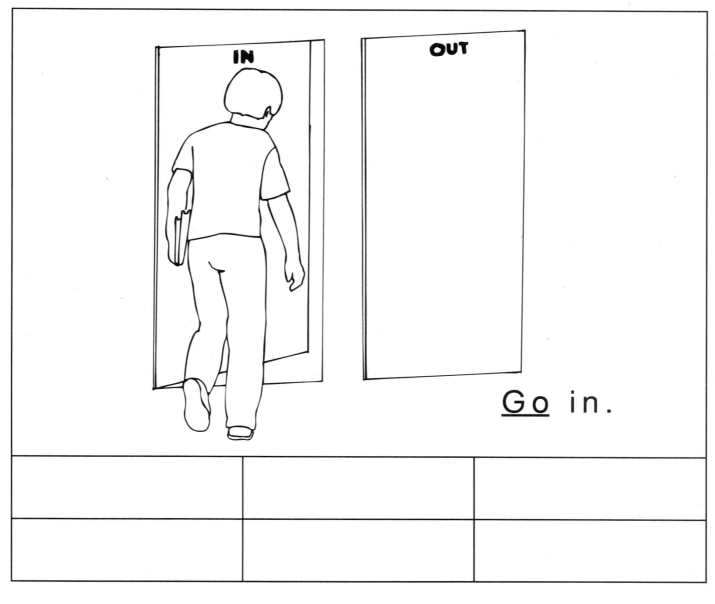

<u>Go</u> in.

| no | so | got | dog | go |
| of | go | go | go | do |

go	go	go
go	go	go

Name_____

Fast   fast

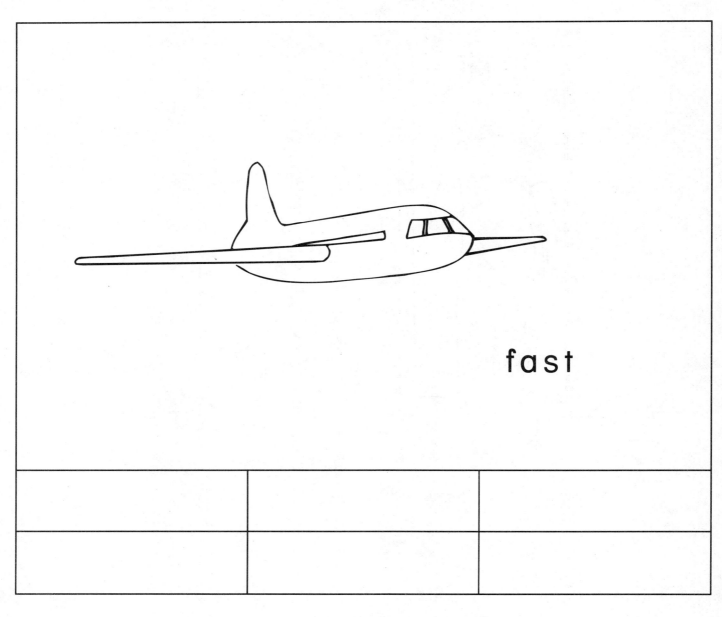

| fist | last | fast | fat | fast |
| fast | fact | fall | lost | first |

| fast | fast | fast |
| fast | fast | fast |

Name_____

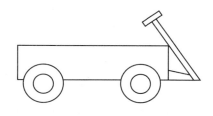	I see oranges in a wagon. A wagon can go fast.
	A tree is green and brown. A tree can run fast.
	A fox can play house. A fox can run fast.
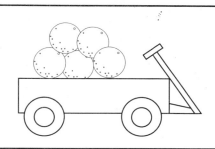	I see oranges in a wagon. Oranges can run fast.
	A bat cannot run. A boy can bat.
	The boy runs under the house. The boy runs by the house.

Name_____

Go fast.

A duck cannot run ☐.

A girl can run ☐.

A fox can run ☐.

A truck can ☐ fast.

A cat can ☐ under a wagon.

A truck cannot ☐ in the house.

| go | go | go | fast | fast | fast |

Name_____

Up   up

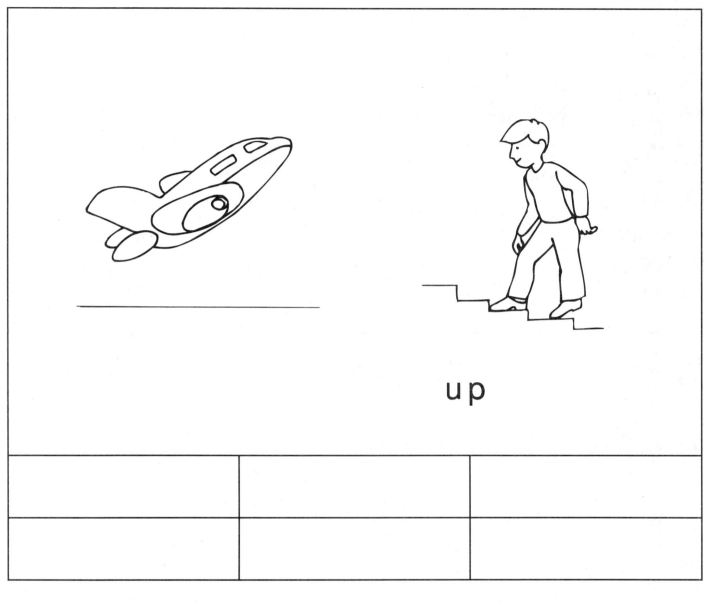

up

| up | pop | pup | up | pun |
| pin | up | cup | up | pan |

| up | up | up |
| up | up | up |

Name_____

The apple _____ up in the tree.
　　　　　　　is　　is not

The cat can run _____ the tree.
　　　　　　　　　up　　under

The girl can _____ up.
　　　　　　　play　　jump

I see oranges _____ in the tree.
　　　　　　　under　　up

The dog _____ run up the tree.
　　　　　cannot　　can

The mouse can _____ under a
wagon.　　　　　　up　　run

Name_____

Down   down

down

| draw | down | dawn | brown | bow |
| down | boom | gown | down | down |

| down | down | down |
| down | down | down |

85/128   Getting Ready for Phonics Part 2. Permission is granted to reproduce for classroom use.   Copyright © 1995 SRA/McGraw-Hill.

Name_____

   go down

go in

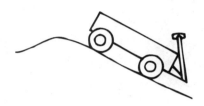   go fast

go down

   go under

go down

   go in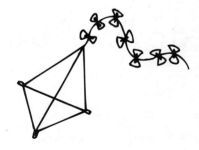

go down

Name_____

Name_____

Can a cat go up a tree?	yes no
Can a duck go up in a tree?	yes no
Can a boy jump up and down?	yes no
Can a truck jump up and down?	yes no
Can a truck go fast?	yes no
Can a boy go fast in a wagon?	yes no
Can a girl go in a truck?	yes no
Can a duck run down a tree?	yes no
Can a cat run in a house?	yes no
Can a fox run fast?	yes no

Name_____

Hill   hill

A boy and a girl play on a | hill |.

| hall | bill | hill | hull | hill |
| hid | hill | hit | hill | his |

hill	hill	hill
hill	hill	hill

Name_____

Can a boy go up a tree?	yes no
Can a boy run up a hill?	yes no
Can a wagon go down a hill?	yes no
Can a hill run fast?	yes no
Can a boy jump under a hill?	yes no
Can a hill jump up and down?	yes no
Can the girl play on a hill?	yes no
Can a truck go up a hill?	yes no
Can trees run on a hill?	yes no
Is a hill blue?	yes no

Name_____
_____

A boy and a girl play on the ☐.

A ☐ is on the hill.

The girl is ☐ the wagon.

The wagon can go ☐ the hill.

The wagon can go down ☐.

The boy can ☐ down the hill fast.

| run | wagon | fast | down | hill | in |

Name_____

Dog dog

dog

day   boy   dog   big   dog
bay   dog   dig   dog   bag

dog	dog	dog
dog	dog	dog

Name_____

dog	duck	boy
dog	draw	boy
draw	duck	dog
boy	truck	boy
dog	duck	blue
bat	down	boy
dog	duck	box

Can a dog run up a tree?   yes   no
Can a boy draw and color?   yes   no
Can a duck jump up?   yes   no
Can a dog run fast?   yes   no

Name_____

Color the dog on the hill black.
Draw a dog by the tree.
Color the duck down by the hill yellow.
Draw a purple X on the hill.
Color the oranges on the tree orange.
Color the dog by the house brown.

Name_____

Treehouse treehouse

 and  is

<u>tree</u> and <u>house</u> is treehouse

treetop   treehouse   treasure   treehouse
trees   houses   treehouse   treehouse

treehouse	treehouse	treehouse
treehouse	treehouse	treehouse

Name_____

Playhouse   playhouse

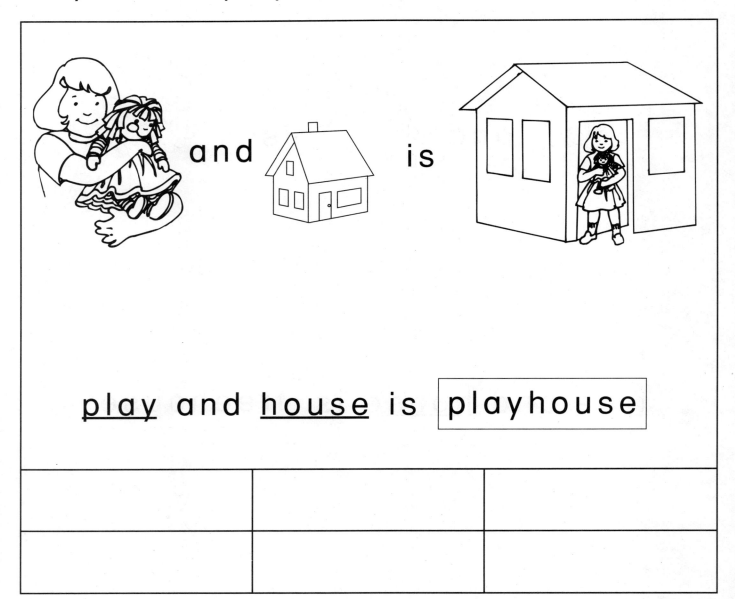

play and house is playhouse

| houses | playhouse | players | playhouse |
| playhouse | playing | playhouse | doghouse |

| playhouse | playhouse | playhouse |
| playhouse | playhouse | playhouse |

Name_____

Doghouse   doghouse

 and  is

dog and house is doghouse

doghouse   houses   dogwood   doghouse
doughnut   doghouse   doghouse   dormouse

doghouse	doghouse	doghouse
doghouse	doghouse	doghouse

Name_____

The dog is ☐ in the doghouse.

The ☐ and the dog play by the house.

The boy and the duck play ☐ the tree.

The cat is ☐ in the tree.

The cat can see the ☐ by the house.

Run fast, dog. ☐ fast!

| dog | up | Run | girl | not | under |

Name_____

Will   will

The dog will go in the doghouse.

will   with   well   will   wit
will   will   win   mill   wall

will	will	will
will	will	will

Name _____

The dog [_____] go in the doghouse.

The boy [_____] go in the doghouse.

The duck [_____] go in the 🌊 .

The cat [_____] go in the 🌊 .

The girl [_____] run up the hill.

The boy [_____] run up the hill.

will	will not	will
will not	will not	will not

Name_____

Will a truck jump up and down?	yes no
Will a dog go in a doghouse?	yes no
Can I see a hill on a tree?	yes no
Can boys run in a treehouse?	yes no
Can I see a tree on a hill?	yes no
Will a doghouse run fast?	yes no
Will a duck play in a playhouse?	yes no
Can boys and girls go in a playhouse?	yes no
Can girls play in a treehouse?	yes no
Can a dog run up and down a hill?	yes no

Name_____

This   this

the   this   is   his   this
these   hiss   this   this   thin

| this | this | this |
| this | this | this |

Name_____

[_____] a hill.

A house [_____] the hill.

[_____] a boy and his dog.

The boy and the dog [_____].

[_____] a girl and a duck.

The duck and the [_____]

run down the hill.

This is	This is	girl can
This is	is on	can play

103/128 *Getting Ready for Phonics Part 2.* Permission is granted to reproduce for classroom use.   Copyright © 1995 SRA/McGraw-Hill.

Name_____

Pond pond

A duck can go in a [pond].

pound   pans   bond   pond   pond
damp   pod   pond   pout   pad

pond	pond	pond
pond	pond	pond

104/128   *Getting Ready for Phonics Part 2.* Permission is granted to reproduce for classroom use.   Copyright © 1995 SRA/McGraw-Hill.

Name_____

This is a ☐.

A ☐ is in the pond.

The boy and girl play ☐ the pond.

The boy and girl cannot go ☐ the pond.

A dog can ☐ in the pond.

A ☐ will not go in the pond.

Color the duck orange and brown.
Color the pond blue.

| by | go | pond | cat | in | duck |

Getting Ready for Phonics Part 2. Permission is granted to reproduce for classroom use.

Name_____

Sand   sand

The boy can play in the sand.

sand   sound   and   sad   sand
send   sand   sang   sand   song

sand	sand	sand
sand	sand	sand

Name_____

Grass   grass

A mouse is in the grass .

guess   rags   grass   grass   grabs
grass   gas   sags   press   grass

grass	grass	grass
grass	grass	grass

Name_____

Draw grass on the hill.
Color the grass by the tree green.
Draw a dog in the grass on the hill.
Draw a red X on the grass by the pond.
Draw a dog by the tree.
Color the house blue.

Name_____

pond	sand	grass
pond	send	grass
pant	sand	press
pond	and	grass
play	sand	gas
pond	sand	green
boy	down	grass

Will a truck run in a pond?   yes   no
Will a duck go in a pond?   yes   no
Will a boy play in the sand?   yes   no
Can a girl run in the grass?   yes   no

Name_____

I see ☐ by the house.

I see ☐ on the hill.

I see ☐ by the pond.

I cannot see ☐ on the hill.

Draw a duck in the pond.

Draw a dog by the pond.

Color the duck yellow.

| grass | grass | sand | sand |

Name_____

oranges in a box	bat under the sand
truck in the sand	sand by the pond
a little house	mouse in the grass
duck in a pond	cat up in a tree
tree by a hill	dog by a doghouse

111/128 *Getting Ready for Phonics Part 2.* Permission is granted to reproduce for classroom use.   Copyright © 1995 SRA/McGraw-Hill.

Name_____

Is a treehouse in the sand?	yes	no
Is grass in a house?	yes	no
Will the cat play in a pond?	yes	no
Will a duck play in a pond?	yes	no
Is grass on a hill purple?	yes	no
Can a dog go in a pond?	yes	no
Will a pond run up a hill?	yes	no
Will a mouse run in the grass?	yes	no
Can a boy play in the sand?	yes	no
Can a girl and a boy go in a pond?	yes	no

Name_____

Get get

The boy will get in the truck.

go   got   get   yet   get
pet   get   gel   get   tag

get	get	get
get	get	get

Name_____

We t   wet

The girl is wet .

wet   met   wit   wed   wet
ten   web   wet   wet   net

wet	wet	wet
wet	wet	wet

Name_____

The _____ is under the ☂.
      boy   girl

The girl _____ get wet.
      will   will not

The boy _____ under the ☂.
      is   is not

The boy _____ get wet.
      will   will not

The little dog is in the _____.
      house   doghouse

The little dog _____ get wet.
      will   will not

Name_____

To   to

The dog runs to the tree.

it   at   out   to   to
to   to   of   too   top

to	to	to
to	to	to

116/128 *Getting Ready for Phonics Part 2.* **Permission is granted to reproduce for classroom use.**   Copyright © 1995 SRA/McGraw-Hill.

Name_____

The truck will go _____ the house.	to	under
The girls play _____ the sand.	up	in
The duck will play _____ the pond.	in	to
The boys will go _____ the treehouse.	to	down
The mouse will run _____ the grass.	to	down
The boy and girl play _____ the tree.	to	under
The cat will run _____ the girl.	to	in
A boy and a dog run _____ the hill.	in	down
Run fast _____ the big truck.	to	down
The dog gets wet _____ the pond.	to	in

Getting Ready for Phonics Part 2. Permission is granted to reproduce for classroom use.

Copyright © 1995 SRA/McGraw-Hill.

Name_____

Into   into

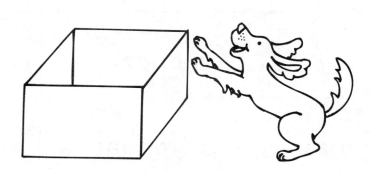

The dog jumps into the box.

onto   into   not   tin   into
inch   until   into   into   undo

into	into	into
into	into	into

Name_____

The truck is _____ the tree.
                      under   into

The doghouse is _____ the grass.
                        on   by

The dog will go _____ the doghouse.
                       under   into

A box is _____ the sand.
             on   under

A cat will get _____ the box.
                 into   down

The boy will go _____ the pond.
                   into   on

Name_____

Mother   mother

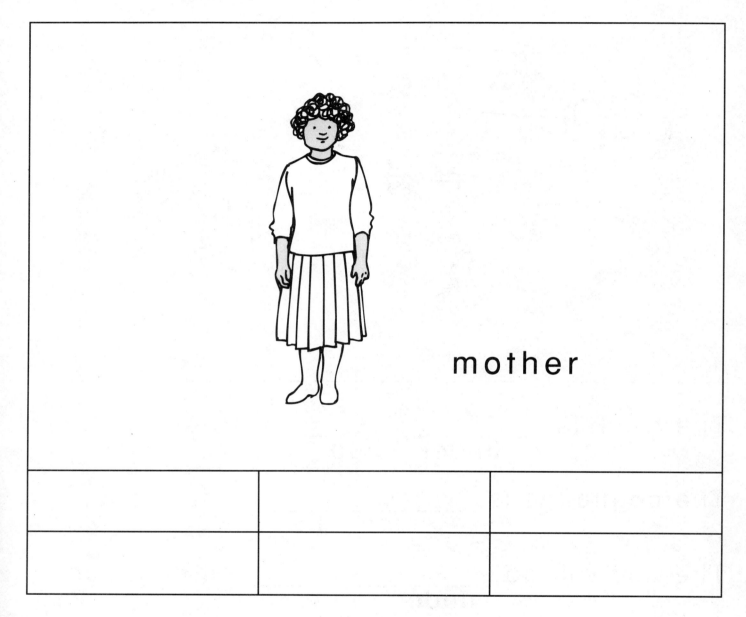

mother   other   another   matter   mother
manner   mother   brother   motor   meter

mother	mother	mother
mother	mother	mother

Name_____

Father father

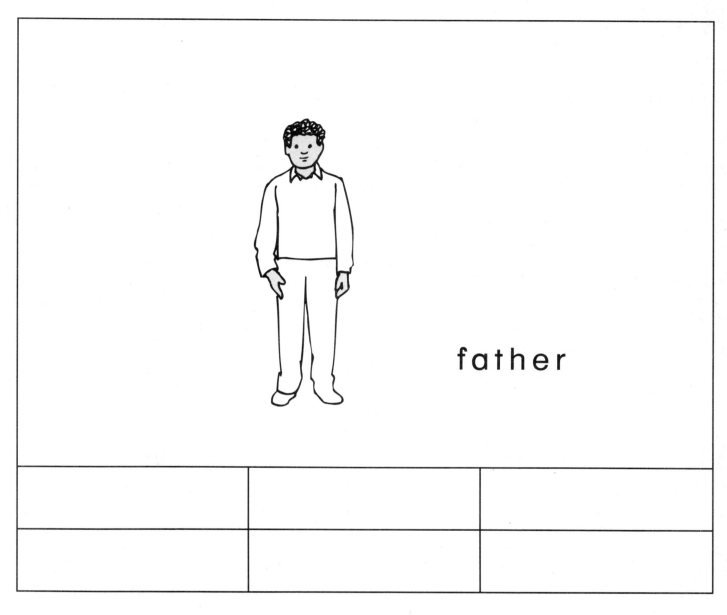

| faster | rather | father | later | fatter |
| father | father | further | father | lather |

| father | father | father |
| father | father | father |

Name_____

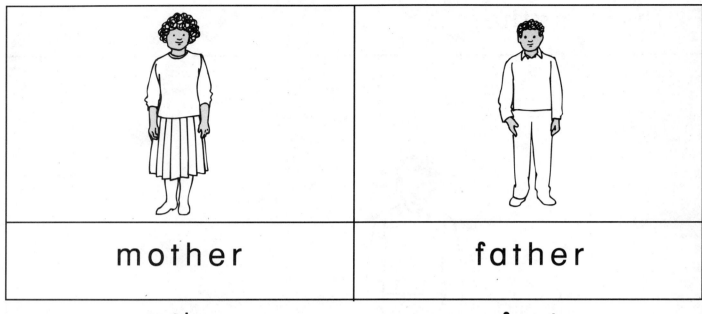

mother	father
mother	fast
mouse	father
mother	friend
master	father
most	farmer
mother	father

Can father go in a truck?   yes   no
Can father play in a doghouse?   yes   no
Can mother go into a house?   yes   no
Can mother jump up into a tree?   yes   no

Name_____

Up in the tree is a _____.

The boys will _____ in the treehouse.

Mother and _____ see the boys.

The big dog is on the _____.

The dog can _____ the boys.

A dog cannot go _____ into a tree.

play	see	Father
treehouse	grass	up

Name_____

Can a dog run to Father?	yes no
Can a duck draw a dog?	yes no
Can a dog get into a playhouse?	yes no
Is a pond wet?	yes no
Will a cat jump into a pond?	yes no
Can Mother run into the house?	yes no
Can sand get wet?	yes no
Is a treehouse down on the grass?	yes no
Will a duck go to pond?	yes no
Will Mother go into a doghouse?	yes no

Name_____

The boy and girl cannot go _____ .
                                                 pond   play

The grass is _____ .
                     wet   red

The tree _____ wet.
                  is   is not

The little dog can go _____ the doghouse.
                                  under   into

The _____ dog is in the doghouse.
     duck   mother

The dogs will not get _____ .
                              wet   will

Name_____

This is a mother duck and a father _____.

Mother duck is in the _____.

I can see _____ little ducks in the pond.

The ducks will get _____.

I can see 2 little ducks on the _____.

Run fast, little ducks. Jump _____ the pond.

Color the ducks orange and brown.

Color the pond and the grass.

| grass | 4 | duck | wet | into | pond |

Name_____

Can a boy see purple sand?	yes no
Will Father play in the doghouse?	yes no
Can a duck get wet in a pond?	yes no
Can a boy jump into a pond?	yes no
Will a mouse go to a cat?	yes no
Can a cat in a tree jump down?	yes no
Can grass get wet?	yes no
Can a mother and a dog play?	yes no
Can boys and girls play on a hill?	yes no
Can a girl run fast up a tree?	yes no

Name_____

It is little.
It can run fast.
A cat can get it.

It is a ⬚ .

It is big.
Father will get in it.
It can go fast.

It is a ⬚ .

It is little.
It is blue and wet.
Ducks go in it.

It is a ⬚ .

It is big and green.
A cat can go up it.
I see apples on it.

It is a ⬚ .

Boys and girls run on this.
It is by houses.
It is green.

It is a ⬚ .

It is big.
It is in a tree.
Boys and girls play in it.

It is a ⬚ .

| grass | truck | mouse |
| pond | treehouse | tree |